Entertaining by the Sea

Rizzoli
NEW YORK

New York · Paris · London · Milan

A Summer Place
Entertaining by the Sea

Tricia Foley
Photography by Marili Forastieri

TABLE OF CONTENTS

OPPOSITE: A few fresh full-blown peony blossoms in a glass container are a wonderful addition to any table setting.

INTRODUCTION

At any time of year, especially in summer, I love pulling out china, glassware, linens, and platters to set the table. With longer days and more relaxed schedules, flowers and greenery in bloom, and farm-fresh produce, it's easy to get friends and family together for a meal, a celebration, or just drinks on the deck to watch the sunset.

Bellport and Brookhaven are magical places on the south shore of Long Island, with views of the bay, sandy beaches, soft marshland—the perfect setting to be spontaneous, to meet up with friends at the beach, the flower market, or the vegetable stand and invite them to dinner that night or lunch the next day. Fresh clams or crabs, a fish someone's caught, and it's a party.

At my house, I am lucky to have an open deck where I've set up an old picnic table and benches for dining and arranged a comfortable sitting area with a big coffee table and white umbrellas for drinks before a meal. It's my outdoor living room and dining room for the summer, and when it gets cooler, I pass out sweaters and we light the heat lamp to extend the season. Watching the sun go down and hearing the waves in the bay are all the entertainment we need.

—*Tricia Foley*

Simple elements that add interest to a summer table setting: a whitewashed canvas runner, a piece of cheesecloth for a plate liner, handblown tumblers and vintage water bottles, bell jars for the cheeses, and "1815" dinner plates and bowls from Royal Doulton.

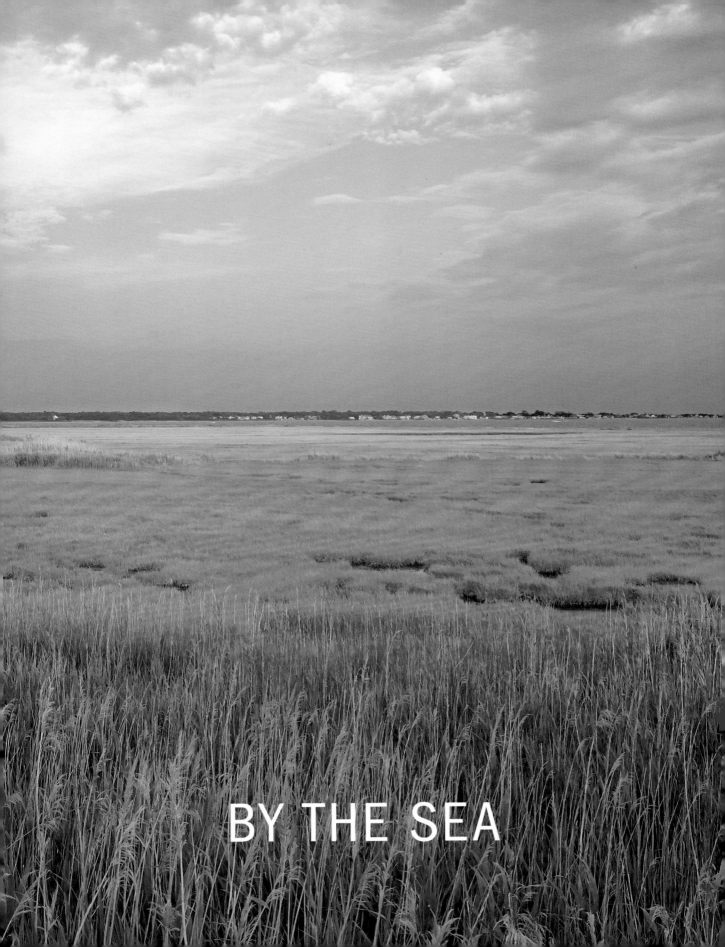

BY THE SEA

SUMMER BRUNCH

When the weather starts warming up in early summer and I can open the doors to the deck and expand my entertaining space, it's nice to gather friends to celebrate the season—especially when I am able to sit outside with a glass of wine or a mimosa and come inside to the set table when ready to eat.

A light, easy-to-prepare menu allows me to be ready for guests and not have to spend time in the kitchen instead of visiting. I love pulling out china and crystal and setting the table with a mix of old and new, modern and classic, and clamshells for salt and pepper. Carafes of water with a sprig of mint or a lemon slice are put on the table. The frittata is easy to prepare if the ingredients are prepped ahead of time. The oven-roasted potatoes with thyme are made in advance, and the salad greens are cleaned and placed in a shallow bowl with white peach slices, but tossed with lemon juice and olive oil at the last minute. Putting the food on the table and passing it around family style is the easiest way to entertain here. And afterward, it's nice to relax over a slice of rhubarb tart and a pot of herbal tea at the table or back out on the deck—it's all about being together and enjoying the view and warmth of the summer sun.

PREVIOUS AND FOLLOWING SPREAD: My house is situated on the marshland in Brookhaven Hamlet, with views all around of the bay and passing sailboats. I've arranged the furniture inside and out to look at the view in this "upside down" house, where the living, dining, and kitchen areas are upstairs and the bedrooms are downstairs. The open-plan space is all windows, and each window frames a beautiful image of the natural environment. **OPPOSITE:** I know it's summer when the peonies start to bloom and my friend Ted welcomes me to his garden with my clippers to cut bunches for the weekend. Simple glass cylinders and single-color blossoms are my favorite. Clamshells are pressed into service as salt and pepper dishes and white stones from the beach hold down napkins when it's breezy.

PREVIOUS SPREAD, LEFT, AND ABOVE: I collect glass bottles and carafes, vintage and new, to use for water, wine, and flowers, and I always have a stack of white, relaxed linen napkins ready for the table in summer.

LEFT: White lacquer trays from West Elm are another staple. I organize glasses on the trays for a bar, set out appetizers on them on different tables, or use them to plate up lunches for laps if we run out of space at the table. Shells are always on the summer tables as condiment dishes, or just because of their natural beauty and soft colors.

MENU

LEMON-FETA FRITTATA

ROASTED YUKON GOLD POTATOES WITH THYME

ENDIVE AND BUTTER LETTUCE WHITE PEACH SALAD

GRILLED PEASANT BREAD WITH WARM RICOTTA,
OLIVE OIL, AND HERBS

RHUBARB-ORANGE TART WITH ICE CREAM

ICED HERBAL TEA

GAVI WHITE WINE

LEFT: A bowl of oven roasted Yukon Gold potatoes with thyme are a nice complement to the frittata. They can be served warm from the oven or at room-temperature. **ABOVE:** I always like to run frittatas under the broiler for a minute or so to puff up and brown the cheese on top.

ROASTED YUKON GOLD POTATOES WITH THYME
Serves 6

INGREDIENTS

2 tablespoons extra-virgin olive oil

2 pounds Yukon Gold potatoes, halved

1 teaspoon sea salt

Freshly ground black pepper to taste

Leaves of 3 fresh sprigs thyme, minced

Preheat the oven to 425°F.

Coat a 9 by 13-inch baking pan with 1 tablespoon olive oil. Arrange the potatoes in one layer on the pan, and season with salt and pepper. Add the thyme.

Drizzle the remaining 1 tablespoon olive oil on top of the potatoes and roast for 30 minutes. Toss the potatoes and return to the oven until golden brown on all sides.

ENDIVE AND BUTTER LETTUCE WHITE PEACH SALAD
Serves 6

INGREDIENTS

1 head Belgian endive

2 white peaches, pitted

1 head butter lettuce, torn into small pieces

Juice of 1 lemon

1 tablespoon extra-virgin olive oil

⅛ teaspoon sea salt

Trim the ends of the endive and cut crosswise in ¼-inch slices. Separate the slices.

Cut the peaches into ½-inch-thick slices.

Toss the endive, peach slices, and lettuce in a large shallow bowl with the lemon juice and olive oil. Sprinkle with sea salt.

LEMON-FETA FRITTATA
Serves 6

INGREDIENTS

1 tablespoon extra-virgin olive oil

8 large eggs

One 4-ounce block feta cheese, cut into small cubes

1 teaspoon grated lemon zest

Handful of fresh mint, torn into small (¼- to ½-inch) pieces, plus extra to garnish

Pinch of red pepper flakes

Preheat the oven to the broil setting.

Coat the surface of an 8- or 9-inch cast-iron frying pan with the olive oil. Heat the pan on medium.

In a large bowl, beat the eggs, then pour them into the hot pan. As the egg mixture cooks, push it from the edge to the center and tilt the pan to let the still-liquid eggs run out to the edges. When the egg mixture is set on the bottom but still soft on top, scatter on the feta, lemon zest, and a handful of mint. Cook until the frittata is set.

Put the frittata under the broiler for a few minutes to lightly brown the top. Cut it into wedges, garnish with mint and red pepper flakes, and serve immediately.

LEFT: A mix of white glasses, from tumblers to goblets, are nice for a summer table setting. **OPPOSITE:** A rhubarb puff pastry tart glazed with orange juice is a refreshing and light summer dessert, especially topped with a scoop of vanilla bean ice cream.

LUNCH WITH A VIEW

As summer days get shorter, the farmstands are brimming with heirloom tomatoes and corn, and it's the last hurrah for local peaches. A small gathering of friends for a simple lunch and a big jug of rosé is the perfect way to spend a Sunday afternoon in early September.

The deck is laid out as a comfortable setting for casual entertaining, and there is also a raised herb garden in the corner for snipping while cooking or garnishing plates. A fringed cotton tablecloth with blue and white stripes, a few pillows against the railing, and rustic wood benches set the scene on the deck for this luncheon with a view of the marshes all around. The menu is created with the day's farmstand finds.

The starter is a slice of old-fashioned tomato tart—simple layers of lush heirloom tomatoes and fresh-made mozzarella with basil leaves placed on top after baking. A salad of mixed greens tossed with lemon and olive oil and sea salt is an easy accompaniment. Penne is tossed with skillet-grilled corn, oven-roasted heirloom cherry tomatoes, thyme leaves, lemon zest, and pine nuts, then sprinkled with Parmesan and red pepper flakes. Grilled peaches with a scoop of vanilla ice cream and a touch of honey are a nice finale. There are great small tabletop grills or hibachis that work well for this, or you can use a griddle on the stove if you don't want to heat up a large barbecue for the occasion.

OPPOSITE AND FOLLOWING SPREAD: A bunch of thistles in lavender blue are the perfect hue for this blue and white table setting looking out to the bay.

MENU

OLD-FASHIONED TOMATO TART
SUMMER HARVEST PENNE PASTA
FARMSTAND GREEN SALAD
GRILLED PEACHES WITH VANILLA
ICE CREAM AND LOCAL HONEY

LEFT: Clamshells found on beach walks make great salt dishes, and I always have small bunches of herbs on the table for guests to add rosemary or mint to any dish. **OPPOSITE:** A collection of vintage glass bottles and vessels hold wine, water, candles, and thistles. The china is Jasper Conran White from Wedgwood, the low glasses for wine are Marta from CB2, and the napkins are indigo linen from West Elm.

PREVIOUS SPREAD, LEFT: A slice of tomato tart is sprinkled with micro greens for garnish. RIGHT: A serving of penne pasta with oven-roasted tomatoes is my one-dish meal, paired with a glass of rosé wine. LEFT AND OPPOSITE: Grilled peach halves with vanilla ice cream and honey are a simple summer dessert. The table grill in white porcelain with a metal liner is by Eva Solo, from Sylvester & Co. Modern General.

PICNIC ON THE BEACH

At the end of my road, a small private beach is the destination for the neighbors to gather and watch the sailboats drift by and for children to play at the water's edge. When the sun is softening it is a perfect time to go with a few friends to the beach with a picnic basket and umbrella for a late afternoon tea. A chambray sheet is a practical beach picnic blanket, as it is cool and sand shakes off easily. I add a couple of chambray pillows to create a comfortable lounging area. Lightweight canvas folding chairs are always ready for such beach visits. I fill my picnic basket with a jar of lemonade garnished with lavender sprigs, a bottle or two of iced tea with mint, and cucumber sandwiches. Sugar cookies and ripe rosé strawberries are an added treat. This easy-to-prepare light fare can stand as a late lunch or early supper. The Brookhaven setting is magical no matter the season, but especially on a warm summer's day.

OPPOSITE: A woven straw picnic basket holds all the fixings for the picnic. Cucumber sandwiches are composed of thinly sliced wheat bread spread lightly with cilantro-lime dressing. Cucumber slices and a sprinkling of microgreens are placed in between. Wrapped in parchment paper and string, they are easy to manage at the beach. **FOLLOWING SPREAD:** I use an oversize canvas tote bag to carry everything to the beach, including a favorite old chambray sheet and pillows. A natural canvas market umbrella and folding chairs are perfect outdoor furnishings. The food is packed in white MUJI stackable tins that fit perfectly in my picnic basket.

MENU

CUCUMBER SANDWICHES
WITH MICROGREENS

SUGAR COOKIES SPRINKLED
WITH GOLDEN SUGAR

ROSÉ STRAWBERRIES

LEMONADE WITH LAVENDER SPRIGS

MINT ICED TEA

ABOVE: Lemonade in a large mason jar filled with ice cubes and sprigs of lavender from the herb garden is a refreshing drink on a hot summer's day. Cream enamel tin cups are durable and easy to manage. **RIGHT:** A bottle of mint iced tea cools off at the edge of the water. I use a stash of glass bottles with stoppers to keep brewed teas chilled, ready for guests who stop by or to put in picnic baskets. **OPPOSITE:** Individually wrapped sandwiches and seasonal rosé strawberries are served on small white plates that are easy to stack and carry in a picnic basket.

VINTAGE BOAT PICNIC

Friends John and Beverly Allan Starke and John's daughter, Annie Starke, have a longstanding tradition of having picnics on their vintage wooden boat on the canal in back of their family home. They make a great team; Beverly, who is an art consultant, loves to create the table and interior settings, and Annie, who is an actress, is one of the cooks in the family. For a late summer afternoon cruise, Annie prepares a menu of toasted tomato-mayo sandwiches, lobster-salad lettuce cups, farmstand radishes with sea salt and butter, and roasted baby eggplant with peppers, but the *pièce de résistance* is a bucket of steamed clams made canal-side in a camping grill pan. The dessert in a jar is a peach shortcake with strawberry sauce and mint.

The 100-year-old classic boat, *Zula*, is an important part of the Starke family history and summer rituals. John and his brother David grew up here and spent summers on the boat, going to the beach, fishing, clamming, picnicking, and, when they were older, having cocktail cruises. Vintage wicker chairs, new cushions, and even an oriental rug dress the boat in style, and a table set with a white linen cloth serves as the buffet. Vintage silver trays and crystal punch cups complement the period of the boat and add a celebratory touch. An invitation to old friends in the neighborhood to spend the afternoon together on the boat for a floating summer picnic is always a treat.

OPPOSITE AND FOLLOWING SPREAD: Annie and Beverly head down to the boat dock using an oar to help with canvas bags and baskets filled with good food and wine for their afternoon lunch.

MENU

FARMSTAND RADISHES WITH
SEA SALT AND BUTTER

BITE-SIZE TOMATOES

ROASTED BABY EGGPLANT WITH PEPPERS

TOMATO AND MAYO SANDWICHES
ON TOASTED WHITE BREAD

LOBSTER SALAD IN RADICCHIO AND LETTUCE

STEAMED CLAMS IN LEMON, SHALLOT, AND
WHITE WINE SAUCE

PEACH SHORTCAKE IN A JAR

OPPOSITE, ABOVE, AND LEFT:
Farmstand radishes, bite-size
tomatoes, and sea salt are an easy
starter, while Annie sautés the
clams on a portable dockside grill,
then garnishes them with fresh
parsley from the garden.

OPPOSITE: Carefully wrapped in brown paper and string, tomato and mayo sandwiches on toasted white bread and roasted baby eggplants with peppers are a summer tradition for the Starkes. **ABOVE:** A bucket of vintage silverware, a jar of minted water, and a stack of napkins held down by a stone are ready for service. Lettuce and radicchio cups filled with lobster salad are nestled in ice chips to keep them fresh in the sun.

LEFT AND ABOVE: Annie and her dad, captain and film producer John Starke, take the boat for a leisurely cruise along the canals in Brookhaven Hamlet while wine is served.
RIGHT: Desserts are readied for the last course. Easy to transport on a tray, jars with chunks of shortcake and peaches are topped with whipped cream, strawberry sauce, and fresh mint leaves.

AT HOME WITH NATURE

A visit to Jon McMillan and Jim Holt's home in Brookhaven Hamlet means driving down a narrow lane through beach grasses to a small wooden house and guest quarters at the water's edge—a sanctuary for birds as well as the owners. The house is nestled into the marshland, with natural unstructured gardens and a deck sited with views of the bay and birdlife.

Jon keeps a camera on a tripod to capture scenes of nature, deer, and the egrets they share this special place with, and he has documented the seasons since they found their home here a few years ago. The deck opens out from the kitchen and dining area, and there is an outdoor table and plenty of flexible seating for friends and family—a perfect outdoor dining/living room for two or twenty.

It is a place for all seasons, but summer evenings are especially magical, with front-row seats to watch the sunset. On the weekends, Jon and Jim host dinner parties with houseguests from New York City, and during the week, friends and neighbors stop by in the evening to enjoy glasses of rosé and conversation, to see the view, watch the moon rise, and talk about what's happening in the neighborhood or in their worlds of architecture, culture, and philosophy. A civilized way to end the day—gathering and enjoying the simple ritual of being together for drinks and good conversation.

This is the best place to wind down at end of day, have a drink, watch the sunset, and catch up with friends.

A winding narrow road through the marsh grass to the beach creates a sense of wonder about what lies ahead—a simple shingled house nestled into the landscape at the edge of the bay, with views of the sea and wild roses growing among native grasses.

FOLLOWING SPREAD: Weathered teak chairs and oversize wicker armchairs get rearranged on the deck depending on the time for sun and sunset viewing. Long Island rosé is the drink of choice for early summer evenings and lives up to its tag-line: "Summer in a bottle!"

An armful of the 'Rosa multiflora alba' roses that grow in the hedgerows placed in a big glass jar of water and a bold black-and-white striped tablecloth create a sense of occasion.
FOLLOWING SPREAD: Nestled in a field of clover, a large cast-concrete and resin shallow bowl functions as a birdbath.

ENTERTAINING FRENCH STYLE

The best French meal in town is always at Chantal Berman's home. Born in the South of France, she has lived in Bellport for many years but hasn't lost her French accent when it comes to cooking and entertaining. Her menu usually includes fresh seafood and vegetables with French flavor, and always a baguette.

Her sunroom is the perfect place for a summer luncheon, with the windows open to the bay breezes and a view of the gardens. The table is a vintage painted metal pedestal surrounded by a mix of strawberry-vine café chairs and others with a sunray motif. It is set with a pale gray-on-white printed floral tablecloth, antique napkins, and sterling flatware and napkin holders from her collection of family silver. A few sprigs of pink anemones in an etched vase are all that are needed as a centerpiece.

The menu is Chantal's ratatouille with summer squash and tomatoes, a roasted pepper dish, and grilled halibut; afterward she serves a simple green salad and chèvre, European style. Her husband, Richard Berman, is the sommelier of the house, and he chose a crisp, cool Sancerre to serve with this light summer fare.

Dessert is a seasonal plum tart with a plate of buttery palmiers on the side for nibbling as the afternoon goes on and the conversation continues at the table . . . drifting between English and French.

OPPOSITE AND FOLLOWING SPREAD: The sunroom setting for this lunch overlooks the garden and the bay. The buffet plates were designed by neighbor Thomas O'Brien for Reed & Barton, a pale gray rendering of berries and leaves called Austin Floral.

ABOVE AND OPPOSITE: Chantal's collection of beautiful hand-painted porcelain dishes and platters, serving bowls and silver are always ready for table settings around the house and garden. A mix of eclectic furnishings all in shades of cream and gray include a narrow buffet table that fits perfectly in the arched window and allows guests to serve themselves.

A velvet-green lawn surrounds the house and runs down to the water's edge; the gardens are filled with topiary hedges and follies. When Chantal is not cooking for friends, she is working in the garden.

MENU

GRILLED HALIBUT
ROASTED PEPPERS
CHANTAL'S RATATOUILLE
SIMPLE GREEN SALAD WITH CHÈVRE
PLUM TART
PALMIERS
SANCERRE WHITE WINE

LEFT: A platter of grilled halibut with an herb sauce, **ABOVE:** A plate of roasted red and yellow peppers. Chantal doesn't follow recipes, but cooks the way her mother and grandmother did—around the seasons, with herbs and white wine, tasting along the way until the dish is just right.

LEFT: A platter of chunky ratatouille, with yellow summer squash, roasted tomatoes, and a bouquet garni for flavor. **ABOVE:** Cubes of marinated mild goat cheese are steeped in olive oil and rosemary, then served with slices of a fresh baguette.

LEFT: A vintage French ceramic footbath is now an oversize wine cooler, with Sancerre bottles chilled and ready for guests.
OPPOSITE: A plum tart on a creamware plate is served along with a dish of buttery palmiers on hand-painted rose dishes with gilt borders.

DINNER ON THE BAY

On a sunny summer evening, Sarah and Gary Wolkowitz gather friends around the pool for drinks and hors d'oeuvres and to watch the sun go down. Then they settle in with everyone at their big table, on the patio under the shade of a large tree, for a relaxed dinner with a view of the bay. The menu is planned around the abundance of fresh farmstand offerings, which are incorporated into the Asian-influenced dishes they favor. The bar is set up with an assortment of drinks: sake, tequila, rosé, and sparkling water. The food is brought out and arranged buffet-style on the long outdoor island by the pool. The table is set with small square white plates, woven mats from Japan, carved coconut spoons from Bali, flutes with straw-wrapped stems, and wooden chopsticks. A large urn is filled with bunches of white calla lilies. Everything is chosen with care and consideration to create a sublime culinary and visual experience. The summer soundtrack—the sound of the waves.

A large square stone table and canvas and wicker seating set the scene for a serene dinner party. Tableware collected from Sarah and Gary Wolkowitz's international trips to the Far East graces the table. **FOLLOWING SPREAD:** A long wooden board serves up rows of Asian lettuce wraps with small bowls of dipping sauces and toppings. Straw-wrapped tall glasses hold chilled rosé.

MENU

ROASTED TOMATO SOUP WITH SOUR CREAM

LOBSTER ROLLS ON BRIOCHE BUNS

ASIAN LETTUCE WRAPS WITH CHICKEN,
SCALLIONS, WATER CHESTNUTS, HOISIN SAUCE,
CARROTS, AND PEANUTS

MIXED VEGETABLE SPRING ROLLS

ARUGULA CAESAR SALAD WITH CORN, TOMATOES,
SHAVED PARMESAN, AND KALAMATA OLIVES

GRILLED PEACHES WITH HONEY AND LIME

DRINKS: ROSÉ, WHITE WINE, TEQUILA,
AND SAKE

A long limestone island is the perfect spot for the bar and buffet. A row of straw stools is great for perching with a drink.

ABOVE: Sarah gathers hydrangeas from her garden to arrange on the outdoor island. **LEFT:** At each setting is a black lacquer tray with a white Japanese square plate and a deep soup bowl of white porcelain set on top. Chopstick stands hold the soup spoons. A sake cup is placed at each setting to offer additional drink options. **OPPOSITE:** Roasted tomato soup is garnished with a dollop of sour cream.

LEFT: The Asian lettuce wraps are filled with organic chicken and water chestnuts and topped with shredded carrots and peanuts and a drizzle of hoisin sauce. **ABOVE:** Mounds of mixed vegetable spring rolls are served on fresh long banana leaves.

LEFT: A summer classic, lobster rolls on brioche buns are served with a seasonal arugula Caesar salad with corn and cherry tomatoes. **ABOVE:** Ripe peaches are grilled with honey and served with lime slices for dessert.

Setting the Table

Gone are the days when the only place to entertain was a formal dining room. Now, a quiet corner in the library, a large hallway, a forgotten patio area, or a porch is inviting, as are chairs pulled up to a kitchen island—all welcoming places to set a table. And a new relaxed entertaining style is a way to express your creativity, whether planning for a large party or a simple meal for two. I like to think of my tabletop collection as a wardrobe, the white china dinner plate the equivalent of the little black dress. Anything goes with it; food always looks good on it. I have a collection of straw placemats for the picnic table, runners for the oval table, white linen tablecloths, and a selection of napkins—from antique damask monogrammed ones to relaxed linen in indigo to red-and-white dish towels used for barbecues or picnics. I have everyday stainless flatware and a set of sterling silver for twelve, as well as assorted antique wood-handled knives and serving spoons, pie servers and salad servers, and wooden boards and platters that add interest and functionality. Glass bottles and carafes and shells for condiments are always on the table in summer. Smooth white beach stones are handy to hold down napkins or put in a jug of flowers if it's breezy. I've collected many pieces in my travels and I love the memory of finding café au lait bowls at a flea market in Paris, a stack of drabware at a Wedgwood sale in England, and chopsticks from a shop in Hong Kong. Having all the elements to entertain at hand makes it easy and pleasurable, which is what it should be.

I usually set up a buffet on the kitchen island. A collection of glass bottles is used for flowers and water for the table.

VILLAGE LIFE

SUNDAY SUPPER AT THE GALLERY

After an art opening at Marquee Projects, the featured artists and friends are invited to the home of the gallery's owners, Mark Van Wagner and Tonja Pulfer, for a celebratory supper, or sometimes Mark and Tonja host a small supper party in the gallery after it closes. Tonja was a caterer in Colorado before she moved to Long Island, and she and her husband, Mark, love to entertain. What better way to do so than to set a long table and benches and continue the conversation about the show with a glass of wine and good food?

Mark is also an artist in his own right, and they found their way to Bellport on a visit to fellow artist John Perreault, who shared their interest in sand paintings. Mark and Tonja liked the community so much that they moved here and opened the gallery to show the art of kindred spirits. They've created a calendar of cultural events, with poetry readings, music, and art performances held throughout the summer in their outdoor green space in back of the gallery—a nice place to sit and visit with friends, drinks in hand. No matter the occasion, food and drink are involved.

PREVIOUS SPREAD: For this evening, a simple white tablecloth, napkins, and dinnerware provide a backdrop for rows of glass bottles filled with bright garden flowers like peonies and foxglove, which complement the art surrounding them. **OPPOSITE:** Lush peonies from the garden welcome guests and have been placed underneath a "coffee" drip painting by John Perreault. **FOLLOWING SPREAD:** Guests help themselves to rosé and platters of delicious food served family style to their art family.

MENU

CAPERBERRIES AND CHERRY TOMATOES
WITH GOAT CHEESE

SLICED TOMATO, MOZZARELLA,
AND BASIL

HOMEMADE BREADS WITH OLIVE OIL AND
BALSAMIC-SPINACH PESTO DIP

ROASTED FENNEL, ORANGE, ARUGULA,
AND FETA SALAD

SIMPLE GREENS WITH RADISH
SLICES AND SEEDS

ROASTED SALMON WITH GRILLED
LEMON SLICES

RICOTTA AND SUN-DRIED TOMATO TART
WITH THYME

RHUBARB AND RASPBERRY COMPOTE
WITH MASCARPONE

SOFIA ROSÉ WINE

SPARKLING WATER WITH MINT

LEFT: Tonja slices heirloom tomatoes from the farmstand to layer in a favorite summer salad of tomatoes and mozzarella.

ABOVE: Roasted fennel with orange slices, arugula, and chunks of feta is tossed with an infused olive oil and vinegar dressing.

LEFT: Mark gilled the lemon slices to accompany the salmon. ABOVE: He keeps the guests' glasses filled with rosé.

RICOTTA AND SUN-DRIED TOMATO TART WITH THYME

Serves 8

This delicious savory tart has been adapted from Yotam Ottolenghi's ricotta tart recipe.

INGREDIENTS

7 ounces frozen pie crust dough, thawed

2 tablespoons unsalted butter

3 tablespoons extra-virgin olive oil

2 medium yellow onions, peeled and chopped

5 cloves garlic, peeled and minced

3 large eggs

2 egg yolks

18 ounces ricotta

2 tablespoons chopped fresh basil

½ teaspoon plus 1 pinch sea salt

½ teaspoon freshly ground black pepper

8 ounces sun-dried tomatoes, plus 3 tablespoons of their oil

6 sprigs fresh thyme

Preheat the oven to 325°F.

Roll out the dough and cut out a circle that is just slightly larger than the base of a 9- or 10-inch tart pan with a removable bottom. Place the pastry inside the pan and refrigerate for 30 minutes.

Cover the pastry with parchment paper and pie weights and bake blind for 15 minutes.

Remove the weights and paper and bake for an additional 10 minutes, or until the pastry is cooked through and golden. Remove from the oven and set aside to cool. Leave the oven on.

Meanwhile, heat the butter and oil in a large skillet over medium-low heat, then sauté the onions and 4 cloves of the garlic, stirring occasionally, until soft but not browned, about 20 minutes. Set aside to cool.

Whisk the eggs and yolks in a large mixing bowl, preferably with an electric mixer, until light and airy.

Fold in the ricotta just until it is incorporated.

Fold in the onion and garlic mixture, basil, ½ teaspoon of the salt, and the pepper, then pour the filling over the prepared crust and bake for 45 to 50 minutes, or until just set.

While the tart is in the oven, in a food processor fitted with the metal blade, roughly chop the sun-dried tomatoes and their oil, the leaves of 3 thyme sprigs, the remaining 1 clove garlic, and a pinch of salt until it forms a chunky paste.

Remove the tart from the oven and immediately spread this mixture evenly over the surface. Then return to the oven for 5 additional minutes.

Remove the tart from the oven, and let cool. Place on a platter garnished with the remaining 3 thyme sprigs. Serve warm or at room temperature.

These small glasses are gallery favorites, used for wine, water, flowers, and desserts. For this dinner party, they are filled with a delicious compote of fresh raspberries and rhubarb layered with mascarpone.

ANTIPASTO AFTERNOON

On a late summer afternoon, under the shade of a big oak tree in Bellport, it feels like the Italian countryside. The top of a big wooden picnic table surrounded by benches and garden chairs—a fig tree in the distance—is laden with platters of the freshest produce from farmstands, and cheeses and cured meats from a local Italian market. The backyard of film editor Camilla Toniolo and film and television producer Harvey Waldman is the gathering place for friends and family for a seasonal feast, Italian style.

The antipasto menu has something for everyone, with ripe tomatoes and peppers, salumi, and cheeses that can be served as an appetizer course, hors d'oeuvres for a party, or on their own as a late lunch or casual supper. A basket of bread, a bottle of the best Tuscan olive oil, and a rustic dish of sea salt complete the menu. Fresh herbs are used to garnish every platter and add fragrance and flavor, and chilled bottles of prosecco and Gavi white wine accompany the meal. The hand-painted ceramic dishes, platters, and jugs are from Deruta, Umbria, collected over the years and mixed and matched on the table with wooden boards and baskets for serving.

In between film projects, Camilla has been known to give cooking classes to friends and neighbors, teaching them to make risotto and frittatas the way her mother and grandmother did when she was growing up in Italy. The results are sampled and savored with Italian wines under the oak tree.

OPPOSITE AND FOLLOWING SPREAD: A simple wooden picnic table and benches under the shade of the tree provide the setting for some of the best Italian meals in town. Friends and family sit around the table and the platters are passed until they are empty.

MENU
ROASTED PEPPERS WITH ANCHOVIES

ASSORTED ITALIAN CHEESES WITH HERBS
PECORINO TOSCANO, SICILIAN
PECORINO, LA TUR FROM PIEDMONT

MOZZARELLA, TOMATO, AND BASIL SALAD

SALUMI PLATTER
CAPICOLA, SALAMI, PROSCIUTTO, CORNICHONS,
ITALIAN OLIVES, SUN-DRIED TOMATOES

CRUSTY PEASANT BREAD
AND SEMOLINA SEEDED BREAD

TUSCAN OLIVE OIL

SEA SALT

GAVI WHITE WINE

PROSECCO

LEFT AND ABOVE: No need for flower arrangements—a basket of fresh basil from Camilla's garden and a ceramic bowl of tomatoes, onions, and shallots add color and texture to the table.

LEFT: Rows of warm slices of home-grown tomato and fresh mozzarella are drizzled with Tuscan olive oil; sprigs of basil are tucked in for serving. **ABOVE:** A bottle of olive oil is ready to drizzle on the semolina bread with a sprinkle of salt, Italian style.

LEFT: On a platter, salumi surround a bowl of Tuscan olives and sun-dried tomato slices. **ABOVE:** Hand-painted Italian ceramic plates are stacked and ready for guests to fill with delicious antipasto selections. **RIGHT:** Camilla likes to put out her favorite cheeses from different regions of Italy for guests to try, including a Piedmontese La Tur and pecorino from Sicily and Tuscany.

RED PEPPERS WITH ANCHOVIES
Serves 6 to 8

INGREDIENTS

4 large red bell peppers

2 tablespoons extra-virgin olive oil, plus more for oiling pan

16 anchovy fillets in oil

2 to 4 cloves garlic, cut into slivers

¼ cup coarsely chopped flat-leaf parsley leaves

½ to 1 teaspoon freshly ground black pepper

Preheat the oven to 375°F.

Slice each red pepper lengthwise into eight strips. Arrange the strips in a single layer, interior sides up, on a baking sheet coated with olive oil.

Drain the anchovies and halve them lengthwise. Put 1 anchovy half on top of each red pepper strip. Sprinkle with the garlic and parsley. Season with black pepper and drizzle the 2 tablespoons olive oil on top.

Roast in the preheated oven until the peppers are slightly softened, about 30 minutes. Serve them warm but not hot.

Note: There is no need for salt because the anchovies are salty enough.

OPPOSITE: Camilla assembles a sampling of her antipasto on a hand-painted ceramic plate from San Gimignano. **RIGHT:** A classic blue-and-white painted pottery dish holds roasted peppers with anchovies, slices of garlic, and Italian parsley.

MIDCENTURY COCKTAILS

Nothing makes Jeff Weinstein happier than the whir of a blender or the cranking of his 1950s ice machine as he makes classic cocktails or creates his own. Formerly a food critic for *The Village Voice* and *The New Yorker,* and author of the book *Learning to Eat,* Jeff turned his talents to researching and creating cocktails a few years ago, and those in the know always look forward to his cocktail parties, co-hosted by his partner, writer Daniel Felsenthal. In their 1950s Popular Science-kit house in the village, they love to serve cocktails at six o'clock, and house Negronis are always on the menu.

Depending on the season, friends gather in the open living room filled with collections of midcentury china or at the table set up in the backyard garden. Hors d'oeuvres can be as simple as small dishes of pickled vegetables, olives, or nuts, or their new favorite: buttered baguette slices with anchovies. Jeff is a "flavor collector," and his pantry is filled with jars and cans of international spices and herbs, bags of Japanese dried seaweed, Mexican jalapeños, and mustards from all over the world. It is a flavor-filled experience to stop by for drinks in summer, when muskmelon daiquiris and basil pesto gin drinks are made with ingredients from the garden.

Jeff likes to set up a table with his collection of glasses—including some with painted diamonds or fruits from the 1940s and Scandinavian colored glass tumblers—and let guests choose their favorites.

MENU

COCKTAILS
HOUSE NEGRONI
GIN PESTO
MUSKMELON DAIQUIRI

HORS D'OEUVRES
ANCHOVIES ON BUTTERED
BAGUETTE SLICES
LIGHTLY PICKLED CUCUMBERS
WITH RADISHES

LEFT: With a drinks station set up, part of the fun is watching Jeff and Daniel produce the cocktails of the evening.
OPPOSITE: Daniel pours the House Negroni from a smoked-glass pitcher.

GIN PESTO
Serves 1

This drink is surprisingly strong. Usually lemon juice is used, but lime juice adds a jump.

INGREDIENTS

12 basil leaves

1 ounce (⅔ jigger) freshly squeezed lime or lemon juice

3 ounces (2 jiggers) gin

½ ounce (⅓ jigger) agave syrup

Muddle the basil leaves in a cocktail shaker.

Fill the shaker with ice and add the lime juice, gin, and agave syrup. Shake well.

Strain the mixture into an old-fashioned glass or any medium-size glass filled with ice.

Jeff makes a muskmelon daiquiri wearing a pineapple-printed 1950s shirt from his vintage wardrobe.

HOUSE NEGRONI
Serves 1

For a large party, place old-fashioned glasses or similar glasses, a pitcher filled with equal parts Campari and vermouth, ice, stirrers, a few jigger glasses for measuring, and mezcal (or gin or tequila) on an open table or bar so guests can mix their own drinks.

INGREDIENTS

3 ounces (2 jiggers) Campari

3 ounces (2 jiggers) red vermouth

3 ounces (2 jiggers) mezcal

Measure Campari and red vermouth in equal amounts into a small pitcher and stir.

Chill in the refrigerator, covered, for a few hours or overnight. The next day, combine with the mezcal and serve over ice.

MUSKMELON DAIQUIRI
Serves 2

This cocktail is a quiet firework and is tasty with or without rum. Serve with wide festive straws. Muskmelon is frequently available on Long Island, but you can replace it with another type of fragrant melon if you're having trouble locating it near you.

INGREDIENTS

6 to 8 scoops ripe muskmelon

2 cups crushed ice

6 ounces (4 jiggers) white rum

3 ounces (2 jiggers) freshly squeezed lemon or lime juice (or 1 jigger of each)

1½ ounces (1 jigger) simple syrup or agave syrup

In a blender, blend the ingredients to a slush. Pour into two cocktail glasses.

The living room shelving is filled with the fruits of years spent collecting the finest designs from the midcentury period, designed by everyone from Eva Zeisel to Ray and Charles Eames to Russel Wright.

EASY DESSERT PARTY

With a small cottage in the village, Anthony Luscia was looking for a way to expand his living and entertaining space. He decided the garage, which was used for storage, would be the perfect place for a new multi-use room that opens onto the patio with sectional seating and a long picnic table. He painted the walls white, enameled a new concrete floor in a putty color, and brought in a few pieces of painted furniture he uses for storage and serving. White outdoor café lights strung around the perimeter make the evenings sparkle.

While working for *Martha Stewart Living* and *Martha Stewart Weddings* magazines, Anthony developed an appreciation for all kinds of celebrations, but he especially loves desserts. A stop at his favorite bakery for a coconut cake and assorted cookies and the chilling of a few bottles of prosecco and it's a party. Using his collection of vintage and modern flatware, china, glassware, and serving pieces and mixing them with driftwood from the beach sets the scene. He and his husband, Rusty James, keep it simple and relaxed for family and friends, but always with style.

OPPOSITE: A vintage gray dresser becomes a buffet to serve the main course—a fluffy coconut cake on a pedestal. **FOLLOWING SPREAD:** A few simple pieces of furniture are easy to move around for other entertaining events, from a long table for dinner to a dessert party like this.

A dish of vanilla meringues and a platter of light crispy angel wings dusted with powdered sugar sit near a two-tiered server holding a boxful of raspberry jam–filled linzer tarts from the bakery.

LEFT: The former garage, once used for storage, has been imbued with seaside style, from white-framed prints of shells to driftwood pieces as sculpture. **ABOVE:** A selection of goodies from the dessert buffet.

LEFT: An old sail with hand-painted numbers is used as a curtain, and a narrow shelving unit now holds platters, vases, and wineglasses. **ABOVE:** Two weathered garden chairs are ready for the party.

ONE-DISH LUNCHEON

The house, known as the red cottage at the end of Bellport Lane, is where owner Jeanette Friedman loves to entertain. She has filled the small house with antiques and textiles from her travels and years of collecting. Born in California, she is also a Francophile, as she taught French for years, lived in France, and has incorporated French culture with a California twist into her home and entertaining style. Although she works in the field of psychology these days, she was also a floral designer in San Francisco, and it shows in her colorful textured arrangements of flowers and food for the table.

Her antiques and furnishings come with memories of her travels and gifts from friends, and she weaves them all together with her love of color and pattern. Her dining table set for four is an old black-painted gateleg style that can extend to seat eight, if needed, with patinated Windsor chairs tucked under it, all by a window overlooking the garden.

A favorite summer lunch in her repertoire is a one-dish salade niçoise, a salade composée inspired by a Julia Child recipe that allows guests to create their own plates with their favorite ingredients, including local Long Island tuna. Chunks of a toasted cheese baguette are the perfect accompaniment. Dessert is a French dish called clafoutis, traditionally made with cherries, that Jeanette customizes with seasonal plums, peaches, and berries, all accompanied by a dry white wine—French, of course.

The little barn-red cottage was formerly a carriage house for a big house up the hill, overlooking the bay. Transformed into a summer home, it is nestled in greenery and gardens and is the last house before the ferry. A screen door allows summer breezes to cool the house.

Jeanette's versatile gateleg table folds up to become a buffet against the windows for drinks parties, opens up to seat four at lunch, and expands to seat eight for a larger dinner party. Here, she sets a summery table with straw mats, light lettuce-green linen, salad plates, and napkins. A sandblasted plexiglass chain sculpture by Peter Menderson is the centerpiece.

MENU
SALADE NIÇOISE
WITH MUSTARD VINAIGRETTE

CHEESE-TOASTED FRENCH BREAD

JEANETTE'S CLAFOUTIS

POUILLY-FUISSÉ WHITE WINE

LEFT: Stacks of colorful printed tablecloths and dishes are ready for the table, and flower bouquets from Jeanette's garden are placed throughout the dining area. **ABOVE:** Embossed lettuce plates and napkins are just right for a salad course. **OPPOSITE:** A collection of shallow vintage baskets adds texture to the wall. Every scene becomes a charming still-life.

SALADE NIÇOISE
Serves 6

INGREDIENTS

2 pounds ahi tuna

2 tablespoons avocado oil, or
any neutral oil

Sea salt

Freshly ground black pepper

2 tablespoons extra-virgin olive oil

2 cloves garlic, minced

18 small new potatoes (about 2 pounds),
boiled until tender, cooled, and halved

2 tablespoons finely chopped flat-leaf
parsley leaves

1 pound haricot vert, trimmed and
blanched

2 sprigs thyme, leaves finely chopped

1 large head frisée, dark outer leaves
removed

1 bunch watercress

1 head butter lettuce, leaves separated

6 eggs, hard boiled, peeled, and cut
into wedges

4 medium garden tomatoes, cut into
wedges

12 Niçoise olives

1 (2-ounce) tin anchovy fillets in olive oil,
drained

Mustard Vinaigrette (recipe follows)

Place a large skillet over medium-high heat
and add the avocado oil. Season the tuna on
both sides with sea salt and black pepper.
Carefully place the tuna in the hot oil and
sear for 1 minute on each side to form a
crust. Remove from the skillet and allow to
cool. Slice into 6 equal pieces.

In a large skillet, heat the olive oil over
medium, then add the garlic. Cook for
1 minute, then add the potatoes and stir to
coat. Add the parsley and stir to combine.
Set aside.

Place the haricots verts in a large bowl and
sprinkle with the thyme; toss to combine.

To serve:
On a large platter, make a bed of the
lettuces, then arrange the tuna, potatoes,
haricot vert, eggs, tomatoes, olives, and
anchovies on top. Drizzle with the mustard
vinaigrette.

MUSTARD VINAIGRETTE
Makes a generous ¼ cup

INGREDIENTS
¼ cup extra-virgin olive oil
2 tablespoons Dijon mustard
Sprinkle of freshly ground black pepper

In a medium bowl, slowly whisk the olive oil
into the mustard. Season with pepper.

*NOTE: Store in an airtight container in the
refrigerator until ready to use, or for up to
3 days.*

CHEESE-TOASTED FRENCH BREAD
Serves 6

INGREDIENTS
1 baguette
¼ cup extra-virgin olive oil
1 cup grated Asiago cheese

Slice the baguette in half lengthwise
and then in 4- to 5-inch pieces crosswise.
Brush the cut sides with olive oil.

Sprinkle the cheese on top, and broil until
golden brown.

A classic salade Niçoise is the inspiration for
this one-dish luncheon—all the traditional
ingredients are arranged in rows so that guests
can create their own custom versions.

JEANETTE'S CLAFOUTIS
Serves 6

INGREDIENTS

2 tablespoons unsalted butter, plus more for the baking dish

3 cups whole milk

6 cups mixed fruit (pitted cherries, blueberries, pitted and chopped peaches, pitted and chopped plums)

¼ cup plus 3 tablespoons Demerara sugar

¾ cup granulated sugar

¾ cup unbleached all-purpose flour

Pinch of sea salt

3 large eggs, beaten

1 teaspoon pure vanilla extract

Mascarpone (or whipped cream or vanilla yogurt) for serving

Preheat the oven to 350°F. Butter an 11 by 11 by 2-inch baking dish and set aside.

In a medium skillet, sauté the fruit in the 2 tablespoons butter until soft, about 5 minutes. Add 1 tablespoon of the Demerara sugar and stir thoroughly. Spread the fruit in the prepared baking dish.

In a large bowl, mix 3 tablespoons of the Demerara sugar, the granulated sugar, flour, and salt together. Add the eggs gradually, until a smooth batter forms. Add the vanilla to the egg mixture. Stir to combine, and then pour the mixture over the fruit.

Bake until golden brown, about 1 hour. Sprinkle the remaining 3 tablespoons of Demerara sugar on top and broil for 1 minute to crystallize. Serve with mascarpone.

With a backdrop of a nineteenth-century painted mural, a jade green painted table is tea-table height. It sits in front of a settee upholstered in blue-and-white ticking stripe, filled with pillows made of vintage toile de Jouy and striped grain-sack fabrics. Dessert is self-serve and includes a baked clafoutis of seasonal fruits and a bowl of mascarpone.

129

TRADITIONAL BREAKFAST

Susan Holmes and Matt Heller recently moved to the village of Bellport, a longtime dream of Susan's. She had seen photos of the village in magazines years ago when she was a magazine editor. She found a classic wood-shingled house on Browns Lane that she renovated, and it is now filled with all their treasures—family silver, a photography collection, and the stacks of art books that make it home for them. Already settled into the creative community here, they love to entertain throughout the house.

When houseguests spend the weekend, the couple enjoys preparing breakfast, served in the kitchen if they have a busy day ahead, or at the set table in the dining room if they have time to linger. Matt makes a relaxed breakfast of scrambled eggs or omelets served with farmstand tomatoes, bacon, and multi-grain toast with peach jam. Pots of traditional French roast coffee are served as the conversation flows.

ABOVE: In the black-and-white kitchen, Matt prepares omelets for the couple's houseguests. **OPPOSITE:** The dining table is set with classic white china and Georg Jensen silverware, and the mimosas are ready; a bouquet of peonies from Good Morning Bellport was a gift from houseguests. Susan's collection of artwork is right at home in the dining room.

GRILL MASTER

George Krauth spends his working life in commercial real estate as a creative director developing adaptive reuse of properties from design to branding, and he applies this "place making" approach, as he describes it, to his own home. When he found his house in Bellport, he transformed a nondescript ranch house into a sophisticated retreat filled with wood and natural materials with character.

Every detail is well-considered, from the Aga stove, which holds pride of place in the kitchen, to the chopping-block table, which was made by his great-grandfather. The kitchen opens to the dining area, with a sofa and pedestal table where friends sit with drinks while he finishes cooking, and is adjacent to the porch and outdoor patio. It all flows together.

The furnishings are from old family homes and custom-made pieces by himself or friends. Stacks of wooden boards and baskets, old mixing bowls, and china are used for serving and preparing food, but George's favorite tools in the kitchen are a stack of Griswold cast-iron pans from his grandmother that go easily from stovetop to oven to grill. The china and glass cupboard was built by his great-grandfather, who was a renowned cabinetmaker in Louisville, Kentucky. Family heirlooms and rustic antiques he's collected over the years coexist here and are treasured in this modern setting.

The barbecue is always ready to fire up at George's house. He designed it from a barrel he found and had it welded to accommodate a grill and handles. It exemplifies his way of entertaining and his love of wood-fire cooking, especially seafood in summer.

PREVIOUS SPREAD: George has places to sit and eat and drink throughout the house, porch, and backyard, and he likes to bring out platters of seafood as they are ready in a modular way. He also assembles a platter of lightly steamed vegetables, which he prefers over serving them raw as traditional crudités.

RIGHT: Here, a settee and chairs pull up to a modern white pedestal table with a selection of plates, flatware, and napkins ready for diners to tuck into the next course.

FOLLOWING SPREAD: Favorite wines from the Willamette Valley, along with coasters with George's Bellport House logo, are ready for guests. The softshell crabs are prepared for grilling.

137

MENU

STEAMED VEGETABLE PLATTER
WITH CLASSIC AÏOLI

ANYA'S CRACKERS

RAW OYSTERS ON ICE

COCKLES ROASTED IN A CAST-IRON PAN

ARTICHOKES WITH LEMON,
BOILED, THEN GRILLED

SOFTSHELL CRABS GRILLED
WITH OLIVE OIL, PAPRIKA, AND CUMIN

LEFT: His pantry is always stocked with tins of tuna and anchovies, chosen as much for their artful design as for their contents. **ABOVE:** He follows his friend Anya's recipe for crackers that complement almost all of his menus.

ANYA'S CRACKERS

Makes about 24 long crackers

INGREDIENTS

- 1 cup coarsely ground whole wheat flour
- 1 cup unbleached all-purpose flour, plus more for work surface
- 1 tablespoon extra-virgin olive oil, plus more for brushing
- 1 teaspoon kosher salt
- Flaky sea salt for sprinkling

Preheat the oven to 350°F. Line two baking sheets with parchment paper.

In the bowl of a stand mixer fitted with the dough hook, or in a large bowl, combine the whole wheat flour, 1 cup all-purpose flour, ½ cup water, 1 tablespoon olive oil, and kosher salt.

Mix on medium speed or by hand until just combined, adding ½ to 1 teaspoon more water as needed to bring the dough together. (The dough should feel stiff, and be relatively dry.)

Beat on medium speed or knead by hand until mostly smooth and elastic, about 15 minutes. (If the dough is sticky, add more flour by the teaspoon.)

Cover the bowl with plastic wrap and let stand at room temperature for 1 hour. (The dough can also be refrigerated for up to 3 days).

Transfer the dough to a lightly floured work surface and cut it into four equal pieces.

Using a floured rolling pin and working with one piece of dough at a time, roll out the pieces as thin as possible without tearing.

Using a sharp knife, pizza cutter, cookie cutters, or biscuit cutters, cut the dough into 3 by 1-inch rectangles, 2-inch squares, or any other shape you like.

Transfer to one of the prepared baking sheets and brush each cracker generously on both sides with oil. Sprinkle the tops generously with sea salt.

Bake, rotating the pans halfway through baking, until the crackers are golden brown and lightly blistered, 10 to 12 minutes.

Remove the crackers and let cool completely.

NOTE: Store the crackers in an airtight container or paper bag (but not a plastic bag) for up to 1 week. If the crackers lose their crispness after storing, transfer them to a baking sheet and reheat in a 300°F oven for 5 minutes.

STEAMED VEGETABLE PLATTER
Serves 6

INGREDIENTS

18 fingerling potatoes

Sea salt to taste

An assortment of raw seasonal fresh vegetables, such as:

1 cup string beans, trimmed

1 cup yellow wax beans, trimmed

1 bunch heritage carrots, sliced if large

1 fennel bulb, cut into wedges

Classic Aïoli, (recipe follows)

Place the potatoes in a large heavy stockpot with 3 quarts of water and salt. Bring the water to a boil and let the potatoes boil until easily pierced, 10 to 12 minutes. Drain the water from the potatoes and let them cool, then cut them lengthwise into thick slabs.

Prepare the other vegetables and steam them separately until tender.

Place chipped ice on a platter and arrange the vegetables on top. Serve with the classic aïoli.

CLASSIC AÏOLI
Makes about 1 cup

The versatile sauce is adapted from a Melissa Clark New York Times *recipe.*

INGREDIENTS

3 cloves garlic, grated or mashed to a paste

1¼ teaspoons freshly squeezed lemon juice, plus more to taste

Pinch of fine sea salt, plus more to taste

1 large egg

1 egg yolk

¾ cup extra-virgin olive oil

In the bowl of a food processor fitted with the metal blade (or a blender), combine the garlic, 1¼ teaspoons lemon juice, and salt. Let the mixture sit for 1 to 2 minutes.

Add the egg and egg yolk and blend until combined.

With the food processor running, slowly add the olive oil in a thin, steady stream. Taste for seasoning and add more salt and lemon juice if needed.

Chipped ice on a large pewter platter keeps vegetables fresh and chilled.

LEFT: A large cast-iron skillet is the right size for grilling cockles from the seafood market down the road. **ABOVE:** A vintage screwdriver is the tool of choice for opening oysters. Lemons are the only condiment needed.

LEFT: With artichokes plentiful and in season, they only need to be sliced in half, with the inner leaves scooped out, drizzled with a good olive oil, and placed on the grill to bring out their flavor. **ABOVE:** Softshell crabs are a southern tradition George brings to Long Island, especially when flavored with olive oil, paprika, and cumin.

SUNDAES ON THE LANE

On a warm summer afternoon or evening, Gail Levenstein loves to have friends over for dessert on her porch after an event or just because she's in the mood. It's a wonderful way to entertain. She serves her favorite caramel sea salt and chocolate fudge sauces with ice cream for sundaes.

Gail lives in a classic white shingled Bellport Lane house and friends stop by on the way to the ferry or when they are out for a stroll. She has proper ice cream sundae glass dishes, long sterling silver dessert spoons, crystal jugs for sauce, and a tray of Champagne flutes at the ready for her ice cream parties. And Gail always has ice cream in various flavors in stock in her freezer to top with the homemade sauces, and she serves each sundae with a glass of festive Champagne. It's like stepping back in time when you sit on her white wicker furniture on the porch and savor an old-fashioned ice cream sundae.

ABOVE: Gail makes classic chocolate fudge and sea salt caramel sauces and puts them in small crystal jugs so guests can use them to top their ice cream. **OPPOSITE:** Her porch dining table is covered in a burlap cloth and is set with straw-embossed plates, sundae dishes, spoons, and a small bouquet of pink peonies. Shown here, a sundae with vanilla bean ice cream and sea salt caramel sauce.

SATURDAY NIGHT DINNER

For Alexandra Lebenthal and Jay Diamond, Saturdays are made for being at home with their children and friends. Saturday night in the summer, they entertain at their Bellport house, which is adjacent to Howells Pond.

Two chickens are put on the rotisserie with vegetables on a tray underneath, salads are made, pies are picked up from the farmstand, and it's a party. Ten to fourteen guests start arriving at about seven p.m. and gather in the kitchen around a charcuterie and cheese board Jay created: a colorful assortment of cheeses, cured meat, fresh and dried fruit, vegetables, and dips, as well as crackers and chips, nuts, olives, and cornichons. There is something for everyone. In the open kitchen, Alexandra puts the finishing touches on the salads: slices of mozzarella and ripe tomatoes with fresh basil and their favorite Caesar salad with kale. The wine is chilled, the table is set, and the candles are lit. They have a few dining areas throughout the house and on the deck that they use when there is a large group.

This dinner is held on the screened porch, where turquoise wicker chairs surround an antique wooden French farm table. Painted pottery dishes and printed napkins are placed on fringed straw placemats, platters are set on the table and passed around family style when the time comes, and friends know to leave room for slices of seasonal fruit pie, the last course.

Alexandra sets the table with round straw-fringed placemats and primitive painted dishes that her mother passed on to her. Colorful printed napkins are the finishing touch. **FOLLOWING SPREAD:** The screened porch is a perfect place to be on a steamy summer evening. Turquoise painted wicker chairs with blue striped cushions surround the antique French farm table.

MENU
CHARCUTERIE BOARD

SLICED MOZZARELLA AND
TOMATO SALAD

CLASSIC CAESAR SALAD WITH KALE

PASTA WITH LEMON AND PEAS

ROASTED CHICKEN WITH CAULIFLOWER
FLORETS AND GREEN GRAPES

CHERRY PIE AND CHERRY GARCIA
ICE CREAM

PREVIOUS SPREAD, CLOCKWISE FROM TOP RIGHT: Late Saturday afternoon, Alex and Jay assemble all the ingredients for their dinner; their mise en place includes all the ingredients chopped and prepared for the pasta dressing and the kale Caesar salad; a sliced mozzarella and tomato salad is prettily arranged; and two chickens are put on the rotisserie to slow roast. **ABOVE AND OPPOSITE:** Alexandra and Jay before the guests arrive. Jay's *pièce de résistance* is an abundant board of charcuterie, vegetables, fruit, and cheeses that is laid out on the kitchen island for guests to nibble at while drinks are being poured and food preparation is monitored.

AN INDIAN FEAST

Maneesh Goyal, co-owner with Priyanka Chopra Jonas of the chic new Indian restaurant Sona in Manhattan, loves to entertain, especially on summer weekends at his home in Bellport. He and his husband, Andrew Wingrove, and their newly adopted son, Adrian, gather friends and family regularly at the table by the pool for relaxing afternoons and evenings. Behind the high privet hedges on South Country Road is a verdant garden setting for this sunny luncheon for six. Maneesh uses his new line of tableware for Sona, Sultan's Garden china, which pairs beautifully with the Panna cream embroidered table linens that are also part of the collection. He fills the table with bouquets of apricot tree peony blossoms and fragrant garden roses. Food from the Sona menu is brought out to share with friends—all the dishes are easy to warm up or can be served at room temperature—and is accompanied by blood orange pomegranate spritzers.

Fresh green-patterned china from Maneesh Goyal's Sultan's Garden collection dresses the table with a mix of brass accessories, all set against Panna cream embroidered linens. The palm tree–etched brass Panna wine cooler does double duty with a bouquet of apricot peonies and garden roses in one compartment and a bottle of white wine in the other.

MENU

INDIAN-INSPIRED GAZPACHO WITH
CILANTRO AND CUMIN

SPRING SALAD WITH SNOW PEAS
AND MINT DRESSING

SPINACH AND GOAT CHEESE SAMOSAS

VEGETABLE BIRYANI

PANEER FLATBREADS

GARLIC NAAN

BLOOD ORANGE POMEGRANATE
SPRITZERS

The porch at the side of the
house is the perfect place
for outdoor dining. Its pergola
roof provides shade for the
table but still lets the sun in.

ABOVE: A tray of refreshing blood orange pomegranate spritzers with sprigs of rosemary await the guests. They can be made with sparkling water or topped up with prosecco. **OPPOSITE:** A bowl of Indian-style chilled gazpacho is spiced with cumin and cilantro. Maneesh likes to add berry sprigs and flowers to place settings and trays.

ABOVE: Maneesh warms up the paneer flatbreads on the outdoor grill. Wedges are perfect to serve with drinks.
RIGHT: The large straw drinks tray has glasses of tequila, an ice bucket brimming with ice, and an assortment of bites, including olives, shrimp, dipping sauce, pistachios, and mini-breadsticks.

LEFT: Goat cheese and spinach samosas sprinkled with seeds are warmed for the guests. In the background are garlic-and-herb-seasoned naan that have been cut into wedges. **ABOVE:** Large, spicy paneer flatbreads are warmed and served with drinks. **OPPOSITE:** Classic vegetable biryani with saffron rice and mixed vegetables is always a favorite.

Flowers and Centerpieces

Pale blue hydrangeas say summer on Long Island to me, whether they are used in big bouquets to fill a simple jug, or as single blossoms in small vases marching down the length of the table. Summer is also the time for peonies—from the palest pink to the deepest fuchsia—and fragrant old-fashioned garden roses add style and grace to a table setting. As summer evolves, what is available from the garden or farmstand changes. Early summer lilac and peony arrangements give way to hydrangea and Queen Anne's lace, marguerites, and dahlias.

Although beautiful hand-blown glass vases add a refined decorative touch, it's always good to have a stash of pretty bottles, odd cups, and old-fashioned jelly jars on hand to fill with casual flowers. Whether from a field or a farmstand, wildflowers placed in a jar are sometimes all you need for a casual table. Driftwood and shells, or smooth white stones, can be used to create a tablescape, which is especially pretty when candles are placed in between for evening light.

A favorite hostess gift, to bring or receive, is a bouquet of seasonal flowers to put on the dining table, bar, or porch. And a nosegay of herbs is always welcome for the table or for using in the kitchen.

A snip of fresh mint in a bud vase, chive blossoms, a stem of geranium, or a spray of fragrant lilacs are easy to place on a table or buffet. I always have a collection of glass vases, carafes, and pottery jugs ready for bouquets or centerpieces of different scales.

COUNTRY LIVING

FARM-TO-TABLE DINNER

It was early days for Mama Farm, and Isabella Rossellini spoke to the guests about her lifelong dream of having a farm with organic vegetables, a cutting garden of flowers, a place for her animals, and more. She partnered with former chef Patty Gentry of Early Girl Farm, who farms two and a half acres of land on Mama Farm and has a CSA and a Saturday morning market. Isabella has also acquired heritage chickens and sheep and now has honey and eggs for sale. Isabella's daughter, Elettra, is managing the farm and expanding the CSA with artisanal breads and organic meat and offering musical evenings and films under the stars.

Isabella travels the world to fulfill her career demands, but as soon as she lands back home in Bellport, her first stop is the farm. The Bellport-Brookhaven Historical Society (BBHS) enlisted New York City chefs who are weekenders in the area, Candy Argondizza and Marité Acosta from the International Culinary Center, and they brought in their troops to prepare the meal, made from local produce. Long Island vintners, including Channing Daughters, Bridge Lane, and Paumanok, supply the wine, and Isabella's local favorite, Blue Point lager, is on hand as well. As the sun is setting and we toast the end of summer, there are smiles all around and requests for the recipe for the last course, an olive oil cake, so we are sharing it here (see page 178).

PREVIOUS SPREAD AND OPPOSITE: Ten tables placed end to end are covered with a continuous length of burlap cloth. The waitresses place glasses, dinner plates, and jars filled with wildflowers from the property's field on the table. **FOLLOWING SPREAD:** Moments throughout the evening showing the crudité presentation, Chef Candy, Joan Kaelin's hors d'oeuvres station, Long Island wine bar, and Isabella seated up on a tractor talking to the guests about her farm.

MENU

CRUDITÉ BASKET WITH BABY CARROTS,
RADISHES, AND BROCCOLI

PARMESAN BLACK PEPPER DIP

SUMMER HARVEST SALAD WITH
TOMATOES, PEACHES, CORN, BASIL,
RED ONION, GOAT CHEESE, FENNEL, AND
CITRUS AND OLIVE OIL DRESSING

TAYLOR'S SOURDOUGH BREAD

MARINATED GRILLED CHICKEN

ROASTED SUMMER VEGETABLES
WITH CURRY SAUCE

FARRO SALAD WITH CUCUMBER, MINT,
BLACK OLIVES, ROASTED RED PEPPERS,
AND SHALLOTS

CITRUS OLIVE OIL CAKE
WITH CRÈME CELESTE AND BERRIES

DRINKS

BLUE POINT TOASTED LAGER

CHANNING DAUGHTERS PINOT GRIGIO
WHITE WINE

2013 PAUMANOK SEMI-DRY
RIESLING WHITE WINE

2013 LIEB CELLARS BRIDGE LANE
ROSÉ WINE

LEMONADE

MINT WATER

OPPOSITE: A mason jar is filled with one large white dahlia blossom, where a cricket has found a home. Glasses are placed mouth-down to keep out any roving insects.
RIGHT: Twine-tied flour sack towels are used for napkins and to hold the flatware. Menus are placed at each setting.

OPPOSITE: Jars of breadsticks are interspersed with wildflowers along the length of the table.
ABOVE: A collection of vintage ironstone bowls are used to serve the farro salad.

CITRUS OLIVE OIL CAKE WITH CRÈME CELESTE AND BERRIES

Makes 12 servings

This light cake was inspired by one served at the New York City restaurant Maialino. A dollop of Crème Celeste, a perfectly tart and creamy concoction, adds an elegant finish. For a gluten-free version, replace the 2 cups all-purpose flour with 4 cups gluten-free all-purpose flour.

INGREDIENTS

Cooking spray for pan

2 cups unbleached all-purpose flour

1¾ cups sugar

1 teaspoon kosher salt

½ teaspoon baking soda

½ teaspoon baking powder

1⅓ cups extra-virgin olive oil

1¼ cups whole milk

3 large eggs

2 tablespoons grated orange zest

¼ cup freshly squeezed orange juice

¼ cup orange liqueur, such as Grand Marnier or Cointreau

Crème Celeste (recipe follows)

Mixed berries, such as blackberries and blueberries, for finishing

Preheat the oven to 350°F. Spray a 9-inch round cake pan (at least 2 inches deep) with cooking spray, line the bottom with parchment paper, and set aside.

In a large bowl, whisk together the flour, sugar, salt, baking soda, and baking powder. In another large bowl, combine the olive oil, milk, eggs, orange zest, orange juice, and orange liqueur and whisk to blend. Add the dry ingredients to the wet and whisk until just combined.

Pour the batter into the prepared pan and bake until the top is golden and a cake tester comes out clean, about 1 hour. Transfer the cake to a cooling rack and let it cool in the pan for 30 minutes.

Run a knife around the inside edge of the pan and invert the cake onto the cooling rack. Peel off the parchment, then flip the cake right side up and allow it to cool completely before cutting, about 2 hours.

Serve each slice with a dollop of Crème Celeste and berries.

CRÈME CELESTE

Makes 3½ cups

This topping is best made a day ahead.

INGREDIENTS

½ cup sugar

1 cup heavy cream

2 cups sour cream

1 tablespoon brandy

In a small saucepan, heat the sugar and heavy cream over medium-high heat until the mixture reaches a simmer and the sugar has melted.

Pour the hot mixture into a large bowl and whisk in the sour cream and brandy to combine.

Transfer the mixture to a bowl, cover tightly, and refrigerate until very cold to set.

BOTANICAL TEA

Artist Lia Chavez does everything with style, designing her own clothing, beauty products, interiors, garden and entertaining settings, and recently a new line of botanical fragrance products called Hildegaard. A few years ago, Lia designed a contemplative garden of herbs for herself, but soon she found herself needing more space, so she rented an acre of land on Isabella Rossellini's farm to produce larger quantities for her new line. She studied with nutritionists and herbalists in developing it and designed her signature packaging and branding with her husband, David Shing.

When Lia was ready to launch the line, she invited a few friends to her home for an afternoon tea and a workshop to sample the product with her special blend of herbal tea and tiny desserts and pastries she created with a local patisserie. Her friends are all involved in some aspect of the fashion and beauty world and followed Lia's cues for flowing cream and white dresses, and she wears a dress from her own Contemplative Garments collection.

The table is set with dreamy layers of gauze and tulle and the tea-ware was created in a collaboration with Mud Australia. The centerpiece is a dramatic tonal arrangement of amaranth and roses, grown locally.

Lia grows herbs for her products at Isabella Rossellini's Mama Farm; here she is in the field cutting flowers for her botanical tea party. **FOLLOWING SPREAD:** She sets the table with a gauzy tablecloth and a centerpiece overflowing with flowers from her garden. Amaranth and roses in fuchsia create a dramatic effect when combined with the white china and teacups. She serves an array of tiny desserts and botanical teas.

MENU

HILDEGAARD STIMULATING
TEA BLEND

CHAMPAGNE

SPONGE CAKES WITH
WHIPPED CREAM, NASTURTIUM BLOSSOMS,
AND ORANGE PEEL

MACARONS: PISTACHIO, STRAWBERRY,
AND ORANGE WITH SPRINKLES

CHOCOLATE WAFERS WITH
MERINGUE FILLING AND PANSIES

TINY PUFF PASTRIES WITH BORAGE
AND VIOLA GARNISH

ICED VANILLA CUPCAKES WITH
AMARANTH SPRIGS

OPPOSITE: Close-ups of black currants and winterberries from the garden; guest Pania Rose samples the botanical tea. All the dinnerware and the tea service were designed with Mud Australia. **ABOVE:** Guests are settled in and enjoying pastries, tea, and the new fragrances Lia has developed.

FROM LEFT TO RIGHT: Iced vanilla cupcakes with sprigs of amaranth. Tiny sponge cakes with whipped cream and nasturtium blossoms. Chocolate wafers with decorative edible pansies. An array of puff pastries is garnished with borage and violets. All are a collaboration with Mademoiselle Patisserie in Patchogue.

SOMETHING FOR EVERYONE

Alanna Stang loves to entertain, and when she cooks up a storm in her blue Brookhaven kitchen, her game plan includes leftovers. With her husband, András Szanto, and two growing boys in residence, as well as visiting family and friends, meal preparation is an important part of life on Beaver Dam Road.

The kitchen has been designed with an open plan that continues to the outdoor brick patio with a long teak table, benches, and chairs that seat twelve to fourteen; pots of herbs create a border around the table.

Grilling is an important part of Alanna's cooking ritual, and a big refrigerator is filled with plastic containers of roasted vegetables, sauces, grilled meats, and salads ready for the next meal. She and her family love to entertain and have many spontaneous, casual dinners and long lazy lunches discussing art and life. Sons Alexi and Hugo love to go clamming at the end of the road and may bring home part of the meal. Bicycling to H.O.G. Farm (stands for Hamlet Organic Garden) down the street brings inspiration for upcoming menus with their CSA offerings of seasonal produce. Large white plates are set on the table with relaxed linen napkins, golden flatware, and glasses filled with snipped clematis from the porch. Platters are set on the table for passing around—service is always family style here.

In a kitchen designed for country living, Alanna prepares for this late afternoon meal; she is relaxed with everything under control. The deep blue kitchen cabinetry is well organized with tableware, serving pieces, and plenty of containers for leftovers.

ABOVE: A long teak table on the brick patio seats ten to twelve, sometimes more, with chairs on one side and benches for little ones on the other. A large white market umbrella keeps guests and food shielded from too much sun. **OPPOSITE:** A full plate with a sampling of everything. **PRECEDING SPREAD, TOP (LEFT TO RIGHT):** Pots of herbs are outside the kitchen for easy access. Blue and white tie-dyed napkins are a favorite. The entrance to the house is through an abundance of hydrangeas. The umbrella centered on the table provides shade on sunny days. **BOTTOM (LEFT TO RIGHT):** Baguette toasts are perfect with a selection of dips. Leftover containers are useful for putting aside food for the next meals. A fresh farmstand salad is always on the table. The barbecue grill is easy to access from the table but tucked away in the hedge.

MENU

APPETIZERS
FAVA BEAN PUREE
ONION CONFIT
TOASTED SOURDOUGH BAGUETTE SLICES
HEIRLOOM TOMATO TART

MAIN COURSE
GRILLED LAMB WITH GREEN HERB SAUCE
ROASTED BEETS WITH OLIVE OIL AND PARSLEY
SMASHED POTATOES WITH HERBS
RADICCHIO AND ARUGULA SALAD

DESSERT
FLOURLESS ALMOND AND ORANGE CAKE WITH
WHIPPED CREAM AND SLICED PEACHES

OPPOSITE: A bowl of seasoned pureed fava beans can be served as a dip for toasted sourdough bread or to accompany the grilled lamb (shown below). ABOVE: A tray of smashed potatoes with garden herbs is served with a large golden spoon, and if any are left, they'll be part of the next day's lunch.

LEFT: Golden and ruby beets are roasted and tossed with olive oil and parsley, a fresh accompaniment to the heartier lamb and potatoes. **OPPOSITE:** Alanna finds this flourless almond and orange cake a great dessert for those with food sensitivities. Whipped cream and peaches are optional.

ANNUAL TAMALE LUNCH

Come midsummer, friends in the know wait for the news that Milan Hughston's tamale order has arrived from Texas. He and his partner, Dennis Miller, put the word out for that weekend and start the preparations. Milan makes a batch of his signature cheese biscuits, gets a large bag of corn and another of tomatoes from the farmstand, and stocks up on Mexican beers and Topo Chico waters. A Sunday lunch or early supper around the pool is the setting for the party.

Platters of cheese biscuits and drinks are served while the tamales are heating up on the grill. A collection of hand-painted Mexican pottery is stacked and ready to be filled with steamed corn on the cob and ripe cherry tomatoes drizzled with olive oil and generous amounts of torn cilantro leaves from the garden. A dessert of Texas pecan pralines from Golden Gals Candy Company in Milan's hometown is the finishing touch. Everything is laid out on a buffet table for people to help themselves, and the bar is set up with buckets of ice keeping the drinks chilled.

ABOVE: A friend brought a basketful of sunflowers, which made a great addition to the table setting. **OPPOSITE, CLOCKWISE FROM TOP LEFT:** A detail of one of the Mexican plates; beef, pork, and chicken tamales laid out on a tray; cheese biscuits from Milan's family recipe are placed on ceramic plates passed around with drinks; a simple salad of chopped local red and yellow cherry tomatoes, drizzled with olive oil and tossed with cilantro leaves.

TURKISH DELIGHT

A Sotheby's auction house executive, Turna Uyar loves to entertain at her Brookhaven Hamlet home, where she celebrates her Turkish heritage by introducing friends to her favorite dishes. Most weekends find her creating vegetable dishes from her garden and the nearby farmstand, and going to the fish market for the freshest fish to grill. Her partner, Jaime Rojas, is in charge of the grill and also keeps the wine flowing. The couple's city life during the week is very different. They are out professionally or with friends every night for drinks or dinner at the newest places downtown or in Brooklyn. But in Brookhaven Hamlet, high heels are left behind, and the dress code is bare feet and summery sundresses.

Part of what Turna enjoys most is setting the table with her daughter, Clea, using her latest tabletop finds mixed with her extensive collection of vintage glassware and wardrobe of colorful tablecloths and napkins. The plates are usually her timeless modern Rosenthal white coupe plates, and the flatware is from her collection of Christofle vintage silver. The glasses can be a mix of pretty cut-crystal and sleek Swedish tumblers. Flowers from the garden or roadside, linen cloths, and napkins are in the color theme of the evening. There is always a soundtrack in the background of jazz or Brazilian music to set the scene, and the night usually ends around the firepit.

An outdoor bar is set up on an old garden table, with a wire tray to organize glasses and bottles. A vintage silver punch bowl chills the wine and a small bouquet of field flowers completes the setting. Stones from the garden keep the etched glasses from blowing over in the breeze. **FOLLOWING SPREAD:** A table set for ten in the field with relaxed linen tablecloth and napkins, jugs of wildflowers holding them down from the summer breezes.

MENU

WELCOMING COURSE

GRILLED CLAMS WITH WHITE WINE, ROSEMARY,
OLIVE OIL, AND BUTTER

GRILLED MEDITERRANEAN SEAFOOD

MEZZE

CHERRY TOMATOES WITH GARLIC AND
POMEGRANATE MOLASSES

GRILLED EGGPLANT

BABY PERSIAN CUCUMBERS WITH YUZU, LEMON,
AND TURKISH SUMAC

SALAD GREENS WITH SCALLION, PARSLEY,
DRIED MINT, OLIVE OIL, LEMON, AND SEA SALT

SUN-DRIED TOMATO DOLMA STUFFED
WITH RICE, CURRANTS, AND CINNAMON

BARBUNYA BEANS WITH DILL
AND LEMON

GRILLED SOFTSHELL CRAB AND SHRIMP
WITH BUTTER, TURKISH RED PEPPER, AND DRIED MINT

MAIN COURSE

GRILLED BRANZINO

GRILLED SCALLIONS AND RED TROPEA
ONION SLICES

DESSERT

HONEYDEW MELON WITH FETA AND A DRIZZLE
OF POMEGRANATE MOLASSES

OPPOSITE, CLOCKWISE FROM TOP LEFT: A platter of grilled branzino with lemon wedges are ready for the table. A plate of honeydew melon and feta with a drizzle of pomegranate molasses is the last course.

Blue-and-white ceramic bowls hold an assortment of vegetable mezze, which are always tossed in olive oil. Turna says, "It helps the digestion and enables guests to drink more wine." The row of mixed patterned blue-and-white bowls are by potter Chloe May Brown. They are filled with cherry tomatoes with garlic and pomegranate molasses, grilled eggplant, barbunya beans with dill and lemon, and baby Persian cucumbers with yuzu, lemon, and sumac. **FOLLOWING SPREAD:** There is always a line for the grilled shrimp, softshell crab, and local clams.

OPPOSITE AND ABOVE: Turna has a wardrobe of tabletop pieces, from a collection of vintage crystal glasses to Christofle hotel silver that she uses for every meal. Her dinner plates are a classic Rosenthal white coupe shape from the 1950s that she mixes in with ease with her Danish candlesticks and the artisanal pottery she collects on her travels, based on the theme of her dinner party. Here she used a blush and apricot color palette and includes napkins from Nicky Kehoe and a linen tablecloth that she buys online from a source in Lithuania.

AROUND THE PIZZA OVEN

A physicist by day, by night Reinhart Schuman is master of the wood-burning oven he built in his backyard in Brookhaven Hamlet. He originally designed it to bake bread, but he can be tempted on a summer's eve to work his magic with homemade pizzas—firing up the oven to create an assortment for appreciative friends and neighbors. He makes his own dough and sauce, and most of the toppings are from nearby H.O.G. Farm and include fresh tomatoes, arugula, potatoes, and artichokes. Some of the pies have red sauce; some are white with herbs. The garden Reinhart and his wife, Ellen Clyne, tend in their backyard by the bay is the perfect spot to gather friends, in this case for a celebration of a neighbor's citizenship ceremony. The pizza boards are put out, the firewood stacked and ready, and the fire is stoked to the right temperature.

Ellen is the gardener in the family, and she has created a small patio garden with seating and borders around the shed that provides a great location for the oven and a buffet table for serving. At the entrance, a big, galvanized tub filled with ice holds different beers and wines, and as guests arrive, they add to the selection and pour themselves drinks. Ellen puts out prosciutto-wrapped melon on skewers, and after everyone is sated with slices of pizza, there are platters of cookies and brownies passed around and invariably there is music—on this evening, patriotic American folk songs in honor of the new citizen in the neighborhood.

Reinhart keeps a collection of boards for pizza presentation. He cuts the pizza with a mezzaluna for easy serving and for guests to help themselves.

OPPOSITE, CLOCKWISE FROM TOP LEFT: The garden setting is lush and green, ready for entertaining; Reinhart puts another variation of his pizza in the oven; the table is set with all the offerings for guests to help themselves; an assortment of pizzas with different toppings, to be drizzled with olive oil, and prosciutto and melon, which are easy to eat. **ABOVE:** A picnic table is filled with pizzas ready to cut and be served.

SUPPER UNDER THE PERGOLA

Isabella Rossellini always wanted a pergola covered in grapevines with a big table under it for long lazy meals like the ones she had growing up in Rome. Here, at Mama Farm, she has made this happen.

Isabella is an active supporter of the organization Friends of Bellport Bay, which seeds indigenous oysters. So these succulent shellfish are always on her menu, along with produce harvested from the farm. Chef Francis Derby is part of the extended family here, and he creates this meal with local seafood and vegetables from Patty Gentry's Early Girl Farm, which is on the property. To start the evening, Francis makes a signature cocktail with Isabella's grapes to accompany with local oysters. The main course consists of vegetable salad and grilled monkfish tails. A dessert of poached local peaches, angel food cake, and whipped cream is the perfect finale.

This table can sometimes seat famous chefs or actors at one end and farmers and artists at the other end, with European friends and family tucked in among them. There is always delicious food and lively conversation.

A weathered old picnic table with benches, set for ten or twelve, bunches of herbs in mason jars and vintage glass bottles and candles on top set the scene for an end-of-summer supper.

ABOVE: A field of wildflowers is a magical backdrop for Isabella's dinners. OPPOSITE: Chef Francis Derby brings a basket tray of grilled oysters to the table of appreciative dinner guests sitting under the grape arbor.

A collection of old clear glass jars and bottles in all sizes hold water and flowering herbs for the table. The white stoneware dinnerware is from Year & Day pottery. Natural linen napkins are tucked under the pasta bowls, with a sprig of sprouted fennel at each place setting.

MENU

FRESH GRAPE AND
FENNEL FLOWER REFRESHER

GRILLED OYSTERS WITH CUCUMBER,
YUZU MALTAISE, AND CHIVE BLOSSOMS

CRUSTY PEASANT BREAD,
FRESH RICOTTA, AND MAMA FARM HONEY

GRILLED MONKFISH TAILS WITH
TOGARASHI PEPPERS AND LEEKS

SUMMER SQUASH SALAD WITH PEACHES,
LOVAGE PESTO, AND PISTACHIOS

CHARRED SPROUTING BROCCOLI AND
SCALLIONS WITH SUMMER HERBS

SAFFRON POACHED PEACHES AND
ANGEL FOOD CROUTONS WITH WHIPPED CREAM
AND ALMOND CRUMBLE

LEFT: Chef Francis made the grape and
lemon refresher with grapes from the
arbor and sparkling water, stirred it with
a stem of bronze fennel, and poured it
over glasses filled with ice.

LEFT: Grilled oysters with a hint of thyme from the farm herb garden are ready to eat.
ABOVE: Another favorite accompaniment, always on the menu, is warm whipped ricotta cheese with a drizzle of Mama Farm honey for dipping crusty peasant bread.

LEFT: A delicious summer salad of yellow squash and zucchini ribbons and peach slices tossed with crushed pistachios. **ABOVE AND OPPOSITE:** One of chef Francis's classic seafood dishes is grilled monkfish tails with sprigs of thyme. **RIGHT:** A mélange of charred scallions, broccolini, and red pearl onions is served on top of the monkfish.

LEFT: Vintage mason jars keep the flatware handy and easy for guests to pass around.
OPPOSITE: Jars of angel food cake croutons layered with poached peach chunks and topped with whipped cream and toasted almond slivers and coconut are ready to serve.

THE PIANO BAR

On a drizzly summer evening, a group of neighbors, consisting of musicians and singers, wander through the garden gate into the weathered, vine-covered cottage with a cello, a guitar, and a songbook, while vodka stingers are being stirred in the kitchen.

Writer and piano enthusiast Bob Morris gathers friends for dinner around an inviting table. Afterward they meander over to the open kitchen, where Bob has taken out the counter stools and installed an upright piano under the counter—"the piano bar"—to enjoy a musical performance.

Dinner can be potluck, a barbecue on the deck, a pizza delivery—it's all about the stingers and the musical menu. For this evening, the table is set with a friend's grandmother's china, Rosenthal's Classic Rose pattern, passed on to Bob. White bistro flatware, assorted tumblers, and soft relaxed napkins are always at the ready. Votive candles are lit on the long wooden table, with its collection of sturdy black-slatted chairs and mismatched cushions. If you squint, you could imagine yourself in a cabin in Maine or rustic cottage in the Carolinas, but it is also classic seaside Long Island.

Architect Elizabeth Roberts holds pride of place with her cello, Bob plays the piano and ukulele and leads the singing, writer Justin Evans plays the guitar, and singers Kristy Hurt, Matthew Doull, Deborah Morosini, and Beverly Allan chime in on American folk songs, Velvet Underground favorites, and Broadway show tunes, sipping martinis and stingers along the way. As Bob's father once told him, "Even when you run out of things to say, you can always sing."

BOB'S STINGER
Serves 1

INGREDIENTS

1½ ounces (1 jigger) vodka

1 scant splash white peppermint schnapps

1 fresh peppermint leaf

Pour the vodka and schnapps into a martini shaker.

Shake and pour into a martini glass. Garnish with the peppermint leaf.

DIRTY BLOODY MARTINI
Serves 1

INGREDIENTS

2 ounces (2⅓ jiggers) vodka

1 teaspoon olive brine

1 splash tomato juice

Drop of hot pepper sauce, such as Tabasco

1 green martini olive

Place ice cubes in a martini shaker. Add the vodka, olive brine, tomato juice, and hot pepper sauce and shake for 30 seconds.

Strain into a martini glass with an olive.

PREVIOUS SPREAD AND LEFT: A mix of elegant martini glasses, etched and cut-crystal, all work together here. The table is set with vintage dishes, votive candles, and brightly colored bistro napkins ready for action. Friends bring garden flowers, like sunflowers, and bottles of wine, and all take turns at the grill or serving family style.

CLASSIC MARTINI
Serves 1

INGREDIENTS

2½ ounces (3¾ jiggers) good gin

½ ounce (⅓ jigger) dry vermouth, or to taste

1 lemon twist or 1 to 3 green martini olives

Place ice cubes in a mixing glass or a small jug. Add the gin and vermouth and stir for 30 seconds.

Pour the mixture into a chilled martini glass, straining out the ice cubes.

Garnish with a lemon twist or olives.

Pantry Basics

One of the keys to easy entertaining is to make it stress-free. Having a well-stocked pantry for planned and impromptu meals is the best way to be prepared. I always have olives, salted almonds, pine nuts, assorted crackers, and truffle chips on hand for last minute drinks and nibbles. For teatime, I keep a package or two of shortbread in my pantry. For quick, simple meals, stock your pantry with different shapes of pasta, good olive oil, and sun-dried tomatoes, and keep pesto and pizza dough in the freezer. Cans of chickpeas and coconut milk come in handy for dressing up soups. As for seasonings, I always make sure to have a supply of the following: hot pepper flakes, Maldon sea salt, and an array of spices and seeds.

I like to store my staples in mason jars as they keep fresher longer. Besides, the jars are ideal organizers. There is no need to confront a messy shelf full of half-empty containers and plastic bags. There is a sense of satisfaction in keeping a neat pantry. You'll then have time to see what's fresh at the farmstand.

Keeping a collection of vintage and new glass mason jars and Weck jars on hand allows staples to be easily identified and decanted. I store pasta on one shelf, crackers and biscuits on another. Teas, nuts, and dried fruit, and flour, sugar, salt, and pepper are on separate shelves. This makes it is easy to locate ingredients quickly.

Recipe Index

This heirloom tomato tart is an easy last-minute luncheon go-to at my house. Prebake a frozen pie crust in a pie pan, then fill with alternating layers of mozzarella cheese and ripe heirloom tomatoes, ending with tomatoes on top. Drizzle with olive oil and sprinkle on oregano and bake for 20 to 30 minutes at 350°F. Top with fresh basil and serve. The better the ingredients, the better the flavor. Served with a green salad and rustic bread, it makes a delicious light summer lunch.

ACKNOWLEDGMENTS

Summer is a special time in Brookhaven/Bellport, Long Island, as its part-time residents spend more time here than they do the rest of the year, and many love to entertain. Whether a large sit-down dinner or a couple of friends for drinks to watch the sun set, these get-togethers are done simply and with style. The farmstands are brimming with ingredients to share with family and friends.

I'd like to thank all the friends who shared their homes, their kitchens, and their meals with us for this book. And thank you to Marili Forastieri, who was always up for our adventures in capturing these stories so beautifully. Doug Turshen and David Huang's design is just right, and Sandy Gilbert Freidus's encouragement and editing are always reassuring. Thank you.

Finally, this book wouldn't have happened without the support and vision of publisher Charles Miers and the exemplary team at Rizzoli—especially senior editor Sandy Gilbert Freidus, production manager Barbara Sadick, executive director of publicity Pam Sommers, and publicist Jessica Napp. Thank you all.

A still-life of white elements for the table—from artisanal pottery to a plaster rose to natural shells and stones found on the beach.

First published in the United States of America in 2023 by
Rizzoli International Publications, Inc.
300 Park Avenue South
New York, NY 10010
www.rizzoliusa.com

Text and photography ©2023 Tricia Foley
Photography by Marili Forastieri

Publisher: Charles Miers
Editor: Sandra Gilbert Freidus
Editorial Assistance: Natalie Danford,
    Hilary Ney, and Tricia Levi
Design: Doug Turshen with David Huang
Design Assistance: Olivia Russin
Production Manager: Barbara Sadick
Managing Editor: Lynn Scrabis

Printed in China

2023 2024 2025 2026 / 10 9 8 7 6 5 4 3 2 1

ISBN: 978-0-8478-9904-3
Library of Congress Control Number: 2022947670

Visit us online:
Facebook.com/RizzoliNewYork
instagram.com/rizzolibooks
twitter.com/Rizzoli_Books
pinterest.com/rizzolibooks
youtube.com/user/RizzoliNY
issuu.com/Rizzoli